Red House

Bexleyheath

Above *Love*: Burne-Jones stained glass in the Passage

Right Woodcut of William Morris by R. Bryden

The beautifullest place on earth

RED HOUSE

Over the Drawing Room fireplace, William Morris inscribed the Latin motto *'Ars Longa Vita Brevis'*, meaning 'Life is short, but art endures'. The words were well chosen. Morris may have lived at Red House for only five years, but the place shaped his life and has had an enduring worldwide influence.

Red House was the only house Morris ever built, and it embodies many of his ideas about art and life. It was also the first independent architectural work of his friend Philip Webb, one of the most important, and underestimated, figures of the Arts and Crafts Movement. The need to furnish Red House inspired Morris to found the interior design firm that bears his name, giving practical expression to his famous demand, 'Have nothing in your houses that you do not know to be useful or believe to be beautiful'. The flowers he planted in the garden helped to shape the first of his wallpaper designs, which have come to epitomise British good taste.

The early years that Morris spent at Red House with his young family were perhaps the happiest of his life. Here he tried to find answers to the insistent question 'How should we live?' Perhaps because of the disappointments of Morris's later life, it was remembered as a dream house – literally so by many of his friends, in whose dreams it regularly reappeared. And his dream of the good life inspired many other communities of artists, not only in Britain, but throughout North America and Europe.

The Pre-Raphaelite painter and poet Dante Gabriel Rossetti described Red House as 'a real wonder of the age … which baffles all description'. More than a century after the Morrises left Red House, it is even harder to reconstruct how it must have been in their day.

This guide makes an attempt, in part by bringing together illustrations of some of the major pieces designed for, but no longer at, Red House.

Red House's rural setting has gone and most of the furnishings have been scattered, but the building itself survives largely untouched. It was cherished by its later owners, in particular Ted and Doris Hollamby, who devoted half a century to protecting it. In 2003 the National Trust, which owes so much to Morris's example as a conservationist, acquired Red House. It intends to encourage wider access of every kind to what Morris's friend Burne-Jones called 'the beautifullest place on earth'.

Above The tiles in the 'Pilgrim's Rest' garden porch are decorated with the medieval form of the letter M (for Morris), together with his motto, a white rose on a sunburst and his coat of arms

Left Red House photographed by Emery Walker in the late 19th century

MORRIS BEFORE RED HOUSE

In January 1853 the eighteen-year-old William Morris went up to Exeter College, Oxford, where he soon made friends with fellow-student Edward Burne-Jones. Amid Oxford's ancient buildings, they fell under the spell of the Middle Ages and of the art critic John Ruskin. After touring the great French medieval cathedrals in 1855, they both decided to dedicate their lives to art.

In 1856 Morris joined the Oxford office of the Gothic Revival architect G.E. Street. Here he encountered the second key figure in his artistic life, Philip Webb, who was working as Street's chief assistant. A few months later, Morris was introduced to Rossetti, who encouraged him to give up architecture for painting. He moved to London to set up a studio in Red Lion Square with Burne-Jones, who had also decided to become a painter, in the Pre-Raphaelite style.

Morris and Burne-Jones returned to Oxford in the summer of 1857, when they were recruited by Rossetti to help decorate the debating chamber of the new Oxford Union with murals inspired by Thomas Malory's tales from Arthurian legend, the *Morte d'Arthur*. Morris himself was chosen to paint the story of the Belle Iseult, the beautiful, doomed lover of Tristram. His contribution was a technical and artistic failure (Morris himself described it as 'extremely ludicrous in many ways'), but the idea of a group of like-minded artists working together remained a potent one, which influenced the decoration of Red House.

In October 1857, while at the theatre in Oxford, Rossetti spotted the seventeen-year-old Jane Burden in the audience. Her pale and solemn beauty appealed to the Pre-Raphaelite imagination, and she was quickly taken up by Rossetti's circle as a model for the Union murals. The following year, she figured as the Belle Iseult in Morris's only completed oil painting. An awkward, but ardent suitor and a clumsy figure painter, Morris struggled to express his growing feelings for Janey in life and in art. On the back of the canvas, he is said to have scribbled, 'I cannot paint you, but I love you.' Morris gave up painting shortly after *La Belle Iseult* was finished; indeed, the picture already suggests where his real talents lay – as a designer. The setting – the canopied bed, the brass jug, the medieval illuminated missal, and the patterned wall-hangings, carpet and table-cloth – also provides a vision of the world William and Janey Morris strove to create together at Red House.

Right William Morris at the age of about 21

Far right *La Belle Iseult*. Morris imagines his wife-to-be in the kind of richly decorated interior they sought to create at Red House

My lady seems of ivory
Forehead, straight nose,
and cheeks that be
Hollow'd a little mournfully.

JANEY MORRIS,
as described in Morris's
Defence of Guinevere, 1858

Top The well from one of the upstairs bull's-eye windows

Above The house is red inside and out: the fireplaces are complex essays in exposed red brickwork

Right The oriel window on the west front

CONSTRUCTING RED HOUSE

Morris found a site for his new home in the autumn of 1858. He chose a spot above the Cray valley, which was still open country – a gentle Kentish landscape of orchards and oast-houses that reminded him of his native Essex.

The place also had deep historical resonances: Chaucer's pilgrims would have passed nearby on their way to Canterbury. Chaucer embodied the Middle Ages for Morris, who was to fill the house with Chaucerian imagery and to christen the garden porch the 'Pilgrim's Rest' in his memory. The tiny hamlet of Upton (now part of Bexleyheath) was also only a short railway journey away from central London.

The first ideas for Red House had emerged that summer, while Morris was on holiday in France with Philip Webb, whom he chose as his architect. Together, they had travelled down the Seine valley from Paris to Rouen, sketching medieval buildings. By April 1859, when William and Janey were married in Oxford, the detailed designs for Red House were complete. Every stage of construction, which took a year, was closely supervised by Webb and Morris, who rented a house nearby while work was in progress. The total cost was £4,000, money that Morris had inherited from his father.

Although Red House was Webb's first commission, so close was the bond between client and architect that Webb understood exactly what was wanted. The result is a complex fusion of Morris's romantic utopianism and Webb's practical common sense, as Rossetti recognised, when he called it 'more a poem than a house … but an admirable place to live in too'.

As in all Webb's buildings, the external appearance of Red House is determined by the internal plan, which is L-shaped, the two wings meeting in a well-lit Staircase Hall, which is the heart of the house. The windows were also placed and shaped to suit the rooms rather than external symmetry, and are a quirky mixture of tall casements, hipped dormers, round-headed sash-windows and bull's-eye windows. Unusually for the period, two of the main rooms are on the first floor – the Drawing Room and the Studio; the only other large room is the Dining Room.

The longer, south range is occupied mainly by the servants' quarters. Webb always paid as much attention to the planning of these areas as to the family rooms. The large kitchen window allowed the staff a view of the garden – a novel feature for the time – but, less successfully, also made the room uncomfortably hot in the late afternoon, when the room was at its busiest.

The Morrises moved into Red House in June 1860. The work of decorating and furnishing their new home could begin.

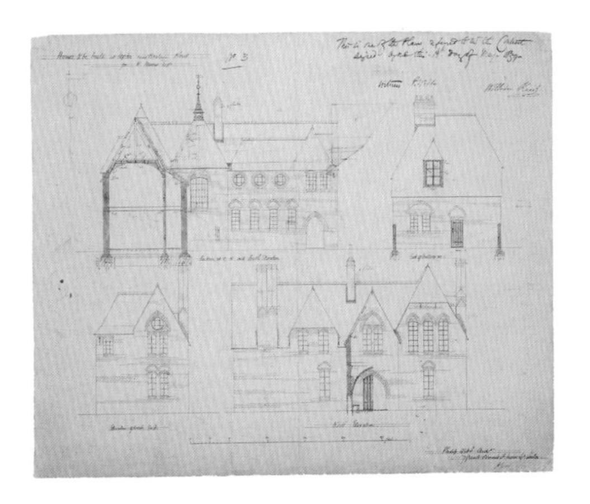

Morris himself described Red House as 'in the style of the 13th century'. The building does feature Gothic pointed windows, but Webb detested any hint of stylistic pastiche or pretence. So he rejected the old Regency fashion for stucco (because it pretended to be stone) and slate (because it wasn't local). He looked instead at the modest red-brick schools and parsonages designed in the 1850s by his master, Street, and William Butterfield, who had been inspired by the commonplace old cottages and barns of the Sussex and Kentish Weald. These kinds of vernacular buildings also encouraged Webb to choose red brick for the fabric and the fireplaces of Red House, and red tiles for its barn-like roof.

Left Philip Webb's 1859 contract drawing for the main elevations of the house

DECORATING AND FURNISHING RED HOUSE

Some of the Morrises' decoration remains, but all of their movable furnishings have gone, and it now takes a considerable effort of the imagination to visualise what these rooms would have looked like in the 1860s. But it was the jewel-like interiors that the Morrises conceived here which represent Red House's novelty and importance.

Decoration

The ceilings of the principal rooms, the Staircase Hall and the main passages were painted with abstract geometric patterns that still look modern today. Burne-Jones was commissioned to cover the walls with murals based on medieval romances and Greek myth. (Morris is best remembered today for his wallpapers, but, in his own time, Red House had none.) Morris filled the windows with new stained glass, which was designed by Burne-Jones and Webb in a medieval style. He also had new tiles painted to decorate the garden porch and several of the fireplaces.

Textiles

The floors were probably covered with Persian carpets, but Morris designed almost all the other textiles himself. Inspired by the Bayeux Tapestry ('very quaint and rude, and very interesting') and the 16th-century needlework at Hardwick Hall, Morris rediscovered the forgotten techniques of medieval embroidery. As Janey recalled, 'He taught me the first principles of laying stitches closely so as to cover the ground smoothly and radiating them properly. Afterwards we studied old pieces and by unpicking etc. we learnt very much but it was very uphill work but only carried through by his excessive energy and perseverance.'

Furnishings

Morris brought with him antique ironwork, armour, enamels and manuscripts he had collected in France, and also the famous 'Prioress's Tale' wardrobe (now in the Ashmolean Museum), which Burne-Jones and Webb had made him as a wedding present. But he found it impossible to buy new pieces that he liked. So he turned to Webb, who designed dressers, tables, beds, chairs, copper candlesticks, table glass, grates and fire-irons specially for Red House – all in a stripped-down Gothic style that suited the other decoration.

The birth of the Morris firm

Morris's difficulties in finding what he wanted to furnish Red House led directly to the foundation in April 1861 of Morris, Marshall, Faulkner & Co., 'Fine Art Workmen in Painting, Carving, Furniture and the Metals'. Thanks to Morris's imagination, energy and wealth, the firm prospered, spreading the example of what had been achieved at Red House across Britain and the world.

Top and above The stained-glass figure of *Fate* attributed to Burne-Jones is set in panels of medieval-style animals designed by Philip Webb

Right Janey Morris's jewel box (now at Kelmscott) was decorated by Lizzie Siddal to resemble a medieval casket

Not a chair, or table, or bed; not a cloth or paper hanging for the walls; nor tiles to line fireplaces or passages; nor a curtain or a candlestick; nor a jug to hold wine or glass to drink it out of, but had to be reinvented.

J.W. MACKAIL, 1899

Above The abstract ceiling decoration in the Studio

Left The Dining Room at The Grange, Burne-Jones's Fulham home. The hanging across the door (illustrated on p.18) came from Red House, and many of the other elements – painted sideboard, Sussex chairs, old carpet, stained glass – give a sense of what Red House would have looked like in the Morrises' time

Morris wanted Red House to be a new kind of building for a new kind of life. When the Morrises first moved here in 1860, they were, like most of their circle, young and recently married, but not yet with children.

Above The Morrises' younger daughter May

Right Janey Morris in a photograph posed by Rossetti in 1865, the year the Morrises left Red House

Opposite above Morris cutting up his daughters' food; a sketch by Burne-Jones

Fellowship is life

LIVING AT RED HOUSE

Morris was a generous host, who believed that good fellowship was essential to the good life. The many weekend visitors to Red House were collected from the station in a horse-drawn wagon, and at once put to work. In the mornings Janey and Burne-Jones's wife Georgiana would work at their embroidery frames or wood-engravings, while the men mapped out the next stage in the mural decorations. In the afternoon, there were carriage rides or games of bowls.

Meals were central to the day. Morris had a prodigious appetite, as Burne-Jones's caricatures make plain, with a particular love for French food and wine. As Georgiana recalled, 'It was the most beautiful sight in the world to see Morris coming up from the cellar before dinner, beaming with joy, with his hands full of bottles of wine and others tucked under his arms.' In the evenings there were old English songs round the piano, and playful high jinks that recalled student days at Oxford. Morris would be relentlessly teased to provoke his sudden rages. On one occasion, he bit a fork so hard in anger that he bent the prongs. There were games of hide-and-seek, and an apple fight in the Drawing Room, which left Morris with a black eye. Georgiana remembered that 'the time we spent together there was one to swear by, if human happiness were doubted'.

This happy bohemian existence still needed staff to support it. The 1861 census lists four live-in servants: Charlotte Cooper (28), cook; Jane Chapman (27), housemaid; Elizabeth Reynolds (31), nanny; and Thomas Reynolds (25), groom. The nanny was taken on to look after the Morrises' children, Jenny, who was born in 1861, and May, the following year. Morris proved a devoted father to his 'littles', as he called them, but inevitably their arrival marked an end to the carefree early days at Red House.

By 1864 the Morris firm had outgrown its first premises in Red Lion Square, and, Morris, weary of the daily commute into London, considered moving the whole business out to Bexleyheath. He also tried to get the Burne-Joneses to join him at Red House, commissioning Webb to design a matching range of buildings to enclose the central courtyard for his friends. But late in 1864 Burne-Jones's young son Philip caught scarlet fever, which he passed on to the heavily pregnant Georgiana. The baby was born prematurely and died after only three weeks. Shattered by this tragedy and worried about money, Burne-Jones decided to pull out of the scheme. Morris and Janey were also both unwell, and their marriage was growing increasingly strained. In 1865 Morris abandoned Red House and, with it, his dream of founding a community of artists living and working together but the dream remained at the heart of the Arts and Crafts Movement that he inspired.

Above Fat and thin: Burne-Jones transforms Morris and himself into stained-glass cartoons

MORRIS AFTER RED HOUSE

Morris moved his family and business back into London, to a large rented house in Queen Square, Bloomsbury. He packed a huge amount into the last three decades of his life. In 1868–70 he published his poetic cycle, *The Earthly Paradise*, on which his contemporary reputation largely rested. In 1871 he and Rossetti took a joint lease on Kelmscott Manor, a mellow stone farmhouse in a remote corner of Oxfordshire which they used mainly in the summer. Many of the furnishings from Red House were eventually brought to Kelmscott, where they remain.

In 1875 Morris reorganised Morris & Co. under his own control and transformed it into both an artistic and commercial success. Two years later, he helped to found the Society for the Protection of Ancient Buildings. Morris's campaign to save Britain's greatest architecture – both grand and humble – directly inspired the birth of the National Trust in 1895 and still guides its work today. He was equally passionate about protecting beautiful landscape from ugly development. The 1880s were largely given up to Socialist politics. In 1891 he set up the Kelmscott Press, which published a lavish edition of the works of his first love, Chaucer, shortly before his death.

Morris never returned to Red House. According to his biographer, J.W. Mackail, he could 'never set eyes on it again, confessing that the sight of it would be more than he could bear'.

Top William Morris painted about 1895 by Cosmo Rowe (Wightwick Manor)

Above The garden at Kelmscott Manor painted by May Morris (Wightwick Manor)

Right Red House painted by the designer Walter Crane after a visit in 1907

RED HOUSE AFTER MORRIS

Although Morris's designs fell out of fashion in the early 20th century, almost all of Red House's later owners respected what he had created here. From 1890 to 1903 it belonged to Charles Holme, a Bradford textile manufacturer who in 1893 financed the setting up of the *Studio*, an influential magazine that supported the Arts and Crafts Movement. From 1903 to 1920, Red House was home to the parents of Edward Maufe, the architect of Guildford Cathedral, whose early work was strongly influenced by Arts and Crafts ideals. A later editor of the *Studio*, Alfred Horsfall, owned Red House in 1927–35, during which period the magazine devoted a special issue to Morris's work.

Throughout the Second World War the house was occupied by the National Assistance Board, which filled the house with ration books. Red House had reached its lowest ebb by 1952, when it was bought by Dick and Mary Toms, in partnership with Ted and Doris Hollamby, for £3,500 – £500 less than it had cost Morris to build the house a century before. Dick and Ted were colleagues in the London County Council Architects Department, which adopted many of Morris's Socialist principles in its pioneering public housing projects for blitzed London. The two families lived happily together at Red House in the same spirit until 1957, when the Tomses were followed by David and Jean Macdonald. They all contributed to a pragmatic, but respectful, restoration of the house. They repaired the roof, preserved the best of the surviving internal features, added Morris & Co. wallpapers and fabrics, and introduced well-designed new furniture from Heals and Ercol. In 1964 the Hollambys became sole owners, and over the next four decades they welcomed the increasing number of Morris enthusiasts who made the pilgrimage to Bexleyheath.

In the late 1990s the Red House Trust was established with the aim of securing a sympathetic future use for the property after the Hollambys' death. Ted Hollamby died in 1999 and Doris in 2003, and their children decided to sell the house to the National Trust to ensure its permanent preservation. It was acquired with generous assistance from benefactors, the William Morris Society and Bexley Council. The Friends of Red House, who have helped keep the place open for several years, continue to act as guides and other volunteers.

Below The L-shaped architect's desk in the Studio was designed by Ted Hollamby for his own use

TOUR OF THE HOUSE

Georgiana Burne-Jones remembered the tall figure of Janey Morris standing alone in the porch to greet arriving visitors. The Latin motto inscribed over the arch can be translated, 'God preserve your going out and your coming in.'

The Entrance Hall
In the 1950s Jean Macdonald repainted the zig-zag pattern on *the front door*, following the existing, but faded, decoration. At the same time Anthony Holloway was commissioned to make the glass mosaic panels symbolising the Seasons, replacing circular leaded glass. David Macdonald made the shelf by the stairs to display flowers from the garden.

The wallpaper (like the others at Red House) is a modern reprint, of Morris's 'Apple' pattern of 1877.

Furniture
The settle-cum-cupboard on the right was designed by Webb specially for Red House. Morris painted the central panels with a scene from Malory, representing *Sir Lancelot bringing Sir Tristram and the Belle Iseult to Joyous Gard.* It includes portraits of Janey (seated, on the left door) and of Burne-Jones feeding a cherry to his wife Georgiana (on the right door). At Red House, Morris was attempting to re-create the Joyous Gard ('Happy Home') of Arthurian legend, but he never finished decorating this piece. It was later partly covered with brown paint; several small areas have been cleaned to reveal the pattern underneath.

The Passage
The glazed screen was added in the late 19th century to reduce draughts. Disciples of Morris who visited the house in later years inscribed their names on some of the panes.

The stained-glass windows are among the earliest surviving examples of Morris glass. Burne-Jones may have designed the figures of *Love* (in red) and *Fate* (blindfolded in green and holding the wheel of fortune), which are surrounded by stylised birds and flowers designed by Webb following 15th-century examples. Burne-Jones's stained glass was to become a mainstay of Morris & Co.

The hanging opposite the windows is a modern reprint of 'Cray', which was one of the last printed textiles designed by Morris, in 1884.

The door at the end of the passage leads into the garden porch known as the Pilgrim's Rest.

Top The entrance porch

Above Philip Webb glass in the Passage

Left The Passage. The wall-hanging is 'Cray', named after a local river

Opposite The Entrance Hall. The painted settle-cum-cupboard is on the right

The Dining Room

May Morris remembered her father sitting here at the head of the table in a great painted chair like an Icelandic warrior. There was no table cloth, and they ate off Staffordshire blue-and-white earthenware plates. They drank from plain, pale green glasses, made for the house by Powell of Whitefriars to Webb's design. Webb also provided beakers and decanters in a more elaborate 17th-century German style.

Morris loved meat, and there was always plenty of beef, mutton and lamb on the menu, followed by fruit from the garden.

The exposed red-brick fireplace is laid in a herringbone pattern, which was to become a popular Arts and Crafts motif. It is filled with Dutch Delft blue-and-white tiles, decorated with traditional patterns and scenes of daily life. These designs, which go back to the 17th century, contributed to Morris's vision of the domestic ideal. As elsewhere at Red House, there is no mantelpiece.

The wallpaper is Morris's 'Sunflower' of 1879. *The hanging* is a modern reproduction of 'Golden Lily', designed in 1897 as a wallpaper by J.H. Dearle, who became Morris & Co.'s chief pattern designer. The Hollambys used this as their main living room.

Furniture

The dresser is another original Webb piece. It is stained and lacquered in 'dragon's blood' red, and has iron handles with a 'tinned' finish. The canopy may have been adapted from medieval ceremonial chairs. It became a favourite motif in Webb's later houses, reappearing, for instance, in the gable ends of the garden front at Standen.

There was also once a canopied settle here (now at Kelmscott Manor). It was again designed by Webb, in ebonised wood with floral panels of embossed, gilded and painted leather.

The Stairs

The staircase is the most dramatic space in the house, flooded with sunlight from windows on two sides, and rising right up into the roof. The stairs themselves are made of oak, with tapered newel posts in a spare medieval style. True to the teachings of Pugin and Ruskin, Webb did not plaster over the load-bearing brick arches or hide the blocks that attached the stair treads to the risers.

Top Delft blue-and-white tiles in the Dining Room fireplace, of the kind Morris loved

Right The canopied settle now at Kelmscott Manor once stood in the Dining Room

Far right The Dining Room dresser was designed by Philip Webb

The embroidered panel depicting Aphrodite, designed by William Morris, is believed to have been worked by his sister-in-law, Bessie Burden, *c.*1859-66. It was intended as one of a set of 12 female figures inspired by Chaucer's poem, *The Legend of Good Women*, devised by Morris for the walls of the Dining Room. The ambitious scheme was never completed and the embroideries of female figures and accompanying fruit trees were dispersed when Morris left Red House. Although the embroidery of the figure is complete, it is unfinished because it has not been cut from the linen cloth and applied to a length of woollen serge as the other surviving embroideries were. This means that the original practice stitches and design sketches are still discernible to the side of the female figure.

The exact provenance of the dining table designed by Philip Webb, *c.*1859-66 is unknown. It is one of only a few surviving Webb dining tables and was probably made under the aegis of Morris, Marshall, Faulkner & Co., the firm Webb co-founded with Morris in 1861. Webb designed two dining tables for Red House but their whereabouts is unknown. This table was acquired in 2007 because of its contemporary date and stylistic similarities to Webb's other furniture made for the house. Morris was an enthusiastic and generous host and Webb recalled in 1898, that he made him two dining tables which were:

Bound round the edge with scoured iron fixed with clout-headed nails, to keep the impatient [Morris] from whittling away the edge if victuals lingered on the road. Doubtless the chill of the iron would be a reminder to hot hands that enough Beaune or Bordeaux had been turned over the thumb.

Letter to Sidney Cockerell, 28 May 1898

The table was acquired with a contribution of £50,000 from The Art Fund, including a contribution from the Wolfson foundation and additional support from an anonymous donor, the J. Paul Getty Jr Charitable Trust and donations to the National Trust.

The ceiling is painted with two abstract repeating patterns; the upper one is based on a traditional arrangement of ceiling joists expressed in reverse. The designs are scored into the plaster as a guide for the painter. The paint, which has darkened with age, is believed to be the original. Morris asked Burne-Jones to decorate the walls with scenes from the Trojan Wars, including 'a great ship carrying Greek heroes'. This scheme was probably never carried out.

Left The Stairs

Right Embroidered panel depicting Aphrodite

Above The *St Catherine* embroidered hanging now at Kelmscott Manor.

Morris may have planned to cover the Drawing Room walls with hangings embroidered in wool and silk with standing figures of famous women, loosely inspired by Chaucer's *Legend of Good Women*, but the scheme was never completed. Alternatively, these hangings may have been intended for the Dining Room.

Right The Drawing Room settle

The Drawing Room

This is the principal living room on the first floor, and, as elsewhere on this floor, the 'wagon' ceiling extends into the roof. The ceiling was originally painted by the Morrises with broad stripes and bands of foliage. In the 1950s Jean Macdonald devised the yellow ceiling decoration over the bay window, which catches the best of the afternoon sun.

The tapering form of the tall red-brick fireplace may have been inspired by those found in French Renaissance châteaux. The Macdonalds added the metal smoke hood in the 1950s.

Furniture

The massive settle was designed by Morris in 1856 for his rooms in Red Lion Square. After it had been installed here, Webb added the canopy and ladder, to create a miniature minstrels' gallery and to provide access to the loft – a typical mixture of the playful and the practical. The upper shelves were originally enclosed by three doors, which Rossetti painted with scenes from Dante as a wedding present for the Morrises.

The bookcases to the left of the settle were designed and made in the late 1950s by Jean and David Macdonald, who at the time were living with the Hollambys at Red House. They also bought the tubular frosted-glass lampshades from the Merchant Adventurers Company in the 1950s.

Murals

Morris commissioned Burne-Jones to paint a cycle of seven *wall-paintings* based on the medieval romance of Sir Degrevaunt, which had been published in 1844. In the event, Burne-Jones completed only three, in the summer and autumn of 1860, and these have deteriorated considerably since then. They represent *The Wedding*, *The Wedding Procession* and *The Wedding Feast.* Appropriately, the royal bride and groom in the final scene (to the right of the settle) are portraits of the Morrises. Below the murals, Morris seems to have painted a repeating pattern of bushy trees, parrots and his *Si je puis* motto in imitation of an embroidered hanging now at Kelmscott. This has long since been replaced by panelling.

The *Broadwood square piano*, *c.*1808–20, once belonged to the Pre-Raphaelite artist Ford Madox Brown (1821–93), who was one of the first visitors to Red House and shared Morris's love of music. It has recently been lent to Red House by Jane and Richard Garnett.

Left ***The Wedding Feast***; one of Burne-Jones's *Sir Degrevaunt* murals in the Drawing Room

Far Left Rossetti's *Dantis Amor* originally filled the central opening of the settle

The Morrises' Bedroom

This would have been one of the most richly decorated and furnished rooms in the house. The walls were covered with blue serge hangings embroidered by Janey Morris. She had found the material in a London shop, and, with her sister, Bessie, worked it with a pattern of daisies taken from a medieval illumination in the British Library. A section survives at Kelmscott.

The room would have been dominated by the huge Chaucer wardrobe (now in the Ashmolean Museum, Oxford), which was made by Webb and decorated by Burne-Jones with scenes from *The Prioress's Tale* in 1857.

In the 1950s, fragments of a mural were uncovered beneath wallpaper. Rossetti's wife Lizzie Siddal is thought to have painted this in the summer of 1861, but was too ill to complete it; she died the following year.

... of al the floures
in the mede,
Thanne love I moste thise
floures whiter and rede,
Swiche as men callen
dayses in our toun.
CHAUCER

These [embroidered hangings] we worked in a simple rough way. The work went quickly and when finished we covered the walls of the bedroom at Red House to our great joy.
JANEY MORRIS

The First-floor Corridor

The barrel-ceiling retains Morris's decoration, which was repainted by David Macdonald. *The bull's-eye windows* still have much of their original glass, which again features Morris's motto. From the windows, you get good views over the garden.

Walk to the end of the corridor and turn left.

The Studio

Morris used this light and airy room as his studio. Ted Hollamby also worked here, at the architect's desk he designed himself to fit the bay window. The ceiling decoration is similar to that in the corridor outside. The Hollambys put up the wallpaper, which is Morris's 'Marigold' pattern of 1875 in a green colourway.

Right The red hanging in the background of this late 15th-century Netherlandish illustration to Froissart's *Chronicles* inspired the 'Daisy' embroidery

Above The bull's-eye windows in the First-floor Corridor are filled with Morris glass

Left The Studio

Opposite above The 'Daisy' embroidered hanging now at Kelmscott was made by Janey for her bedroom at Red House

A most cheerful place it was, with windows looking three ways and a little horizontal slip of a window over the door.

GEORGIANA BURNE-JONES ON THE STUDIO

I know a little garden-close
Set thick with lily and red rose,
Where I would wander if I might
From dewy morn to dewy night,
And have one with me
wandering.

WILLIAM MORRIS

Above and right Morris's 'Daisy' and 'Trellis' wallpapers were inspired by the garden he created at Red House

THE GARDEN

From the start, Webb conceived the house and the garden as a unity. The house was built in an orchard, and he was careful to retain as many of the old trees as possible, which included apple, cherry, oak, ash, yew, hazel and holly. Webb's designs for the house specify that it should be clothed in traditional climbers such as roses, white jasmine and honeysuckle. Late 19th-century photographs show that the walls were soon smothered by ivy.

Morris laid out the garden with a rectilinear arrangement of wattle trellis, softened by informal planting of old flower varieties, of the kind to be seen in medieval *millefleurs* tapestries. As a visitor in 1863 recalled, 'The surrounding garden divided into many squares, hedged by sweetbriar or wild rose, each enclosure with its own particular show of flowers; on this [west] side a green alley with a bowling green; on that, orchard walks and gnarled old fruit trees.' The luxuriant and relaxed mood of the Morrises' garden is perhaps best evoked in Burne-Jones's drawing *The Backgammon Players* of 1861, which includes a porch and trelliswork similar to those at Red House. In the same spirit, May Morris remembered the poet Swinburne lying in the orchard, his long red hair spread out on the grass, as she and her sister Jenny sprinkled rose petals on his face.

The Red House garden was as influential as the house. Morris was fascinated by the patterns made by growing plants, and the flowers in his garden inspired designs such as 'Trellis' of 1862, his first wallpaper pattern. Morris's use of traditional native flowers and his pioneering of the garden 'room' were both to be major influences on the Arts and Crafts garden.

The detail of Morris's planting no longer survives, but the overall shape of his garden, enclosed by its original red-brick wall, remains little altered. In the early 1950s Doris Hollamby rescued the garden from a near-derelict state and gradually replanted it in the spirit of William Morris, preserving his elderly fruit trees where possible.

The Stables

These were built by Webb at the same time as the house, and have 'a kind of younger-brother look with regard to it', as Georgiana recalled. Webb also designed a traditional country wagon for the Morrises. They employed a groom, Thomas Reynolds, to look after their two horses.

Above The garden today

Below Burne-Jones's *The Backgammon Players* of 1861 evokes the mood and planting of the Red House garden